"For everyone who has felt the thrill of lifting off and setting it back down safely!"

Table of Contents

Remote Control Helicopters

By

Hey! This is Easy!

Introduction

Whether you are new to the world of remote control helicopters or a seasoned veteran, let me be the first to welcome you to this great hobby!

It is always best when you can write about something you love and we have loved RC copters for years now. There is just something really cool about being at the controls over something a hundred feet overhead and watching it respond to your direction. It's just a great feeling.

This book is designed to get you started in this great hobby and to get you comfortable with learning how to choose the best copter for your needs and becoming comfortable with flying it. We do not claim to be experts and we aren't employees of the company just writing stuff to sell helicopters. We are just people like you who enjoy going outside (or inside as well!) to fly our helicopters and just have fun.

RC Helicopters is a great hobby because you can start small and at a very small price and grow as you want to whenever you are ready. But that first little helicopter will still be fun and you will still find yourself flying it around your house and having a great time! Look at other pages on this site for helpful information regarding all shapes and sizes of Remote Control RC Helicopters.

We will help you find the size and type that's right for you and we will help you find it at the very best price, too!

There is just so much to know and so much to learn. We can help you enjoy this hobby even more if you will just give us the chance. We look forward to becoming great fellow helicopter pilots!

RC Helicoptering
Overview

Before we get started, I want to take a few
minutes to talk about RC Helicopters as a
hobby. I think it is important to understand
what RC helicopters are all about and why we
fly them around like little kids on Christmas
morning. With a smile on our faces and a gleam
in our eyes.

Never lose sight of the fact that this hobby is
supposed to be FUN. Yeah, it's supposed to be
fun. It's not about who has the biggest or most
expensive helicopter, it's all about who is
having the most fun! If you are not having fun
flying your helicopter, then really, what's the
point of flying it at all?

We have fun by making things fun. That
means choosing the right helicopter for you at a
particular point in your learning curve and
doing things in such a way that it stays fun and
doesn't get frustrating.

Trying to do too much or go too fast too son can ruin the fun and make the entire process frustrating and difficult. But if you approach things in the right manner, you will have a ton of fun!

RC Helicopters cost money. Like every other hobby, stuff costs money to get. But I don't care if you own your own company and make millions of dollars a year, start small with one of the inexpensive smaller copters.

Nothing is fun if you break something 47 seconds into your first flight. The smaller copters are flexible and you can crash them and fly into things and they will bounce right back with little or no damage. The bigger copters are not so forgiving and will break and cause you anger and frustration. So learn on the little guys and move your way up.

Fun also means being careful and practicing certain safety precautions. No one comes home with one less finger and says it was a fun day! Be respectful of those fast spinning blades and watch out for others, including pets during your flights. Don't do crazy or foolish things that may make you regret them later. Have fun but don't go crazy in the process.

Fun also means enjoying yourself in the process. Flying might be tense in the beginning but as you get experience and start to feel comfortable it will get to be more and more fun. Don't get frustrated if you can't fly well after the first day. Odds are that you won't.

EVERYBODY crashes when they are learning. If someone tells you they never crashed, they're lying. Everyone crashes during their learning. Even experienced pilots crash now and then.

Keep things simple and so them slowly and allow yourself to learn. Have fun and congratulate yourself as you see yourself improving. This is not a contest to see who can learn faster. It is a hobby designed to let you have fun and relax. So think of it that way.

Everyone is different and everyone will look to get different things our flying their copters. Some might only be happy when they see their copter 100 ft up doing rolls and other fancy acts. Someone else might be thrilled watching their min copter fly around the den after work. Whatever works for you, that's what you should pursue.

Remember, you should be having fun. Give helicopter flying a chance. It's a cool hobby and very relaxing. Just take it slow and relax. Get that smile on your face and keep it there. That, my friend, is what flying is all about.

Rules, Regulations & Insurance

Like everything else in today's world, there are rules and regulations that we all need to understand and play by. This chapter will deal with a few of the common issues you might need to be aware of. Keep in mind that every state and town has their own laws and ordinances and you should make inquiries to find out if they apply to or affect you. Do NOT think that if something isn't mentioned here you do not need to worry about it! The purpose of these pages is just to get you thinking!

Regulations

In my town, and in the town where I was raised, it is illegal to fly remote control airplanes or helicopters in schoolyards and public parks.

Part of the reason was noise and the other the safety of the people using those areas.

So if you have a favorite place you want to fly your new copter, make a few inquiries to make sure it has not been banned by local or state government.

Even if the area you want to fly is approved for helicopters, use common sense and do not fly when there are other people around. If you want to fly at a local schoolyard do so after school or on the weekends. Even if the playground is empty, do not use it to fly during school hours. You will provide a distraction for the kids and the teachers and the school will not become your best friends!

Another area you should check out is whether or not you have to have a license to fly an RC aircraft in your area. While I do not believe this to be a widespread requirement, it might be in your area. You can check with local government or even a local hobby store that sells helicopters or airplanes can give you information.

Always remember that ignorance of the law is not an acceptable defense if you are caught. You are expected to know and understand all the rules and requirements in your area. You are expected to fulfill and abide by them or risk a fine or worse. Do yourself a favor and make a few calls to make sure!

Insurance

Insurance might be an important consideration, or even a requirement, for you before you start flying your helicopter.

If your local town requires a license to fly your helicopter, you could be forced to purchase insurance as this might be a requirement in order to get the license.

Insurance protects you and others from damage or injury caused by your helicopter. For example, if your copter loses control and flies through Mrs. Brown's large picture window, your insurance would cover the repairs. If it also flew through the window and hit Mrs. Brown while she was having her morning coffee, insurance would cover her injuries as well.

You can check with your current insurance company to see if you can get a rider on your existing policy or even a policy just for the helicopter. It should not be expensive and could save you from a large settlement down the road.

Always make it a priority to know the rules and regulations wherever you fly your copter. If you take it on vacation with you, check the local laws to make sure you are in compliance. Failure to do this might cause you to be fined and even have your equipment confiscated.

You should also check to make sure there are not different rules and regulations for gas vs. electric models. Certain locations might ban gas or nitro models but allow electric copters. They might do this because of noise and environmental factors. Again, make a few calls and check this out.

All of this is useful information to have even before you get into the hobby.

After all, if you can't use any local areas to fly and have to drive long distances in order to enjoy your copter, you should know that before you buy it, right?

One Blade or Two?

When you get past the really small remote control helicopters you will be offered the choice of models with one set or main rotors and ones with two sets of overhead rotors. It is important that you realize the difference before you make your decision.

The problem with overhead rotors is the very turning of the rotors tends to make the body turn as well. The result is the body of the helicopter will continue to rotate as the blades turn. The way this is corrected is by the addition of a tail rotor which creates air movement in the opposite direction to stabilize the body. Helicopters with tail rotors are more difficult to fly and require finer tuning and attention. Because of this they usually require more space as well.

Remote Control Helicopters with two sets of blades compensate for this effect by have two sets of blades spinning in opposite directions. This eliminates the tendency for the body to turn due to blade movement. The force of each set of blades opposes the other set. The two sets of blade rotate in opposite directions and are pitched the opposite way to aid in lift off and landing.

Today most of the midsized and small remote control helicopters use the dual bladed setup. They are very stable and this is an economical ways to make the copter. When you get to the bigger copters, they will have a tail rotor. Ease of flight favors the dual bladed models but true "purists" like the appearance of the single bladed models. They look more realistic as they mimic what a real-life helicopter looks like.

Since space is a consideration you should decide where you are likely to fly your helicopters. If you have limited space available, stick with the two bladed copters. If you have a lot of wide open area, the single blade would be an option after you become more experienced. If you are teaching your kids, or if this will be primarily used by young people, I would recommend the dual bladed models unless your kids are really advanced at flying remote control helicopters. This will save you some big bucks in the long run!

I suggest learning to fly helicopters using the two bladed models and then, after you have the hang of that, step up to the larger double bladed models and finally to the single blade models. This will allow you to minimize damage and learn without ruining helicopters or your bank book! The single blade units seem to be priced higher than the dual blade models and this is usually because of the additional mechanisms required for the tail rotor and other factors. If you just like to have fun flying your helicopter, go dual blade. If you are into realism and don't mind the extra effort in flying, try your hand at a single blade chopper. But only when you're ready!

The Two Primary Systems

There are two primary control systems for RC Helicopters. Those are either **Infra-Red (IR) or Radio Frequency (RF).** There are distinct differences between the two which we will explain here.

Infra-Red (IR) helicopters operate via a beam of light. While you cannot see the light, the helicopter has a sensor on it that receives data from the controller via a beam of light. There are a few advantages and disadvantages of this kind of system.

First of all, this is the system used by most of the small and inexpensive helicopters. That is because it is cheaper to manufacture than the more complicated RF systems. The range for IR systems is much shorter than RF systems, typically around 30 feet max. This might seem short but since most of the small copters are used indoors, 30 feet is more than the size of most rooms. Plus, at 30 feet you lose perspective of distance and you wouldn't feel comfortable flying something that far anyway. You would be afraid of hitting objects or flying into things. So 30 feet is pretty decent for a small copter.

A positive is there is no antenna required at the receiver for IR units. Just a blunt red sensor at the top. For young flyers this is good because there are no sharp metal antennas sticking up that could injure you. This might sound a little foolish but it is an important safety consideration when you have toddlers around.

You also cannot be in another room or behind a wall with IR systems. Although why anyone would think they can fly a helicopter without looking at it is beyond me! You must always have a direct line of sight between you and the copter. It will likely work if the copter goes behind a sofa or something but you cannot control it through walls. This is important to know and understand. So if you are looking to fly helicopters from remote locations as part of spy training or something, IR is not for you!

IR units have another advantage and that is the size of the components required to make an IR receiver in the copter itself. IR requires fewer and smaller components so they can fit inside those really small micro copters and allow them to work. So if you have your heart set on one of the micro copters, be aware you may have no choice except for IR. But since micro copters are highly sensitive to wind it is likely you will be flying them inside anyway so this may not be a big deal.

The largest drawback of IR systems is that they usually cannot be used outside in sunlight. This is usually not an issue as the smaller copters are almost always flown inside. But if it is a calm day and you want to go outside, IR just won't cut it. Reception and control will either be non-existent or spotty at best. You don't want to be flying your copter and all of a sudden watch it go haywire and you can't do anything about it! So if you definitely want to take the copter outside, you will have to buy a larger one and go with an RF unit.

I have an IR copter and it works very well. Do not confuse or judge it based on the $10 toy copters. Those have limited functionality and it is more about making it cheap than it is about the IR system itself. A good IR copter will have a ton of functionality and will do almost anything you normally would ask it to.

Radio Frequency (RF) systems have more functionality and a lot more range than IR units have. You can go into another room, behind a wall, and the range is much, much greater. You can expect 100-200 feet of control range with a good RF remote. The drawbacks are they are more costly and take up more room in the radio controlled helicopter as well. This makes them suitable for the larger copters but not the little ones. RF units have a certain number of channels ranging from 3 to 6. The more channels the more the copter will be able to do and the higher the quality is likely to be. But when you increase quality and functionality, you also increase price.

Both systems have advantages and disadvantages. I think as long as you stay away from the discount store $10 copters you will find IR units a pleasure to fly and available at a very reasonable price point. As you get more experience and go up in size, then go to an RF unit where you will have more control and functionality. But in the beginning when crashes are many and damage is bigger concern, go small and go IR.

Small, Medium or Large?

Remote Control Helicopters can be flown by just about everyone. In other words, there is something for everyone and something you can fly just about anywhere as well.

For the very young among us there are very small helicopters that have built in gyros that are very easy to fly. That is what I first started with and within a few minutes I was able to take off and land and do some basic turns and maneuvers. That is important for beginners because if it is too difficult they will lose interest and never really get the thrill of watching their helicopter flying 100 feet over their heads in an open field. For the very, very young there are really inexpensive helicopter but they are difficult to control and are not really great to learn with.

The great thing about the small copters is that they can be flown indoors. when you are first learning, flying indoors is preferable because you don't have to worry about wind gusts and other things that are present outside but not in your home. Flying inside can be done on rainy days and give you something exciting to do instead of watching television. Flying inside is also good for practicing take offs and landings. Just draw a small circle on a piece of paper and place it on the floor. Fly your copter around and practice landing within the circle.

Medium sized helicopters are more expensive and more difficult to fly although the ones with gyros built in are very stable. The rule of thumb is the bigger the copter the larger area you need to fly it. You would not crank up a large bird in your living room! As you go up in size you will often have the choice between single bladed copters with tail rotors and dual bladed models without a tail rotor. The ones with the two blades are more stable and easier to fly and are recommended for novice flyers. Single blade with tail rotors are more difficult to fly and require more space as well. They are also usually more expensive.

The really large helicopters are the most expensive and naturally take more space to fly. They are definitely not intended for indoor use. They are also more prone to damage because they weigh more and when they crash there is a harder impact. Never try to learn on a large copter. You will crash it and spend money on new blades and rotors and body parts. Start smaller and work your way up to the big boys.

That is one of the reasons why remote control helicoptering is such a great hobby. The little micro helicopters and the smaller ones do almost exactly the same things as the big boys do so you can have a lot of fun inside or in a small space as you can with the larger ones. You can get started on a small budget to test the waters to make sure you like it and then move up in size and quality! But you will still break out the little ones from time to time and take them for a spin! It is that much fun!

Gas or Electric?

There are two types of helicopter out there; gas and electric. The vast majority of the small and medium sized remote control helicopters will be electric and you pretty much have no choice in those sizes. But larger sized models can be available in both configurations. With gas models there is a gas engine in the helicopter and you store fuel on the copter. The remote control system is still electric and you still have batteries that require charging to control the helicopter in flight. But the engine is powered by fuel.

There are two views on the gas vs. electric issue. Some people like the electric models because they are easier to use and fly. There is no loading of fuel or transport flammable fuel from home to the fly site. You also don't have to store the fuel in your basement or garage. For some that can be a significant issue. Especially for people who live in apartments.

With electrics you just switch them on, put them down and then use the remote control to start flying. There are no engines to prime, glow plugs to warm up or anything that you need to do with gas models. They are just easier. Sound might be a problem as well as the gas models are much louder than their electric counterparts. If you are going to fly in populated or residential areas, the noise might get you in trouble. Especially if you have a big backyard and want to fly there. Your neighbors might complain.

Some gas or nitro helicopters have limitations on how high they can fly. This is because the mixture of air to fuel changes as you go higher. Also, gas engines have emissions and therefore are much dirtier. Figure on spending some time when you get home cleaning of engine vapors from your helicopter. Electrics do not have this problem.

If you are going to have the copter used by children, remember that gasoline engines get very hot and can burn you when you touch them after a flight. You also probably do not want them messing with fuel either. Electric models are a much safer way to go when young people are involved. If your children are going to use a gas powered copter make sure you train them thoroughly and teach them to have respect for both the engine and the fuel.

Electrics, though, have a problem with limited flight time. You do not want to load the stuff in your car, drive to a local field, unpack and then fly for 8 minutes and have to pack up and go home again. There is little fun or enjoyment in that. With gas copters you can refill and be back in the air as long as your control batteries are charged enough. Electrics have to be recharged for a few hours on some of the larger ones. For others it could still be 45 minutes. Only solution for that would be to purchase spare batteries. This works well if the battery is easy to switch out on your copter. You can fly, swap out the battery and be on your way in minutes. Batteries are somewhat cheap and are rechargeable. Having a few spares can get you a lot more time in the air.

If you really like the smaller helicopter, they are not that expensive but you really cannot easily change the battery. In that case, you could always just purchase a second copter and fly one while you charge the other. That works well when you have a friend or one of your kids who likes to fly as well. You can fly your copters together and then relive your flight while they recharge!

I'm not sure if there are any studies on this or not but I would almost be willing to bet that electrics are more reliable as well. There is a lot of heat and stress on a gas engine and a lot more parts as well. Which means there is a lot more to go wrong. I'm sure there are a lot of loyal gas copter flyers who have had no trouble and I have nothing concrete to base my opinions on but it just makes sense.

I am not trying to discourage anyone from flying the type of copter they want. My only purpose in writing this page is to make you aware of certain things as they pertain to each type so that you can make up your own mind and get the one that will provide you the most enjoyment and the best results. After all, you are in this for the fun of flying, right?

Which Manufacturer Should I Buy???

    This is kind of like the question "Should I buy a Ford or a Toyota?" There are a lot of manufacturers out there who make remote control RC Helicopters. Most of them are in Japan which doesn't really mean much these days since most electronics and hobby products are made there.

    There are many different types and styles and colors and the choice is mostly personal taste and preference. Technology is technology and almost all of the comparably sized units will perform well as long as they are approximately the same age. I would go with features and looks when making your decision but caution you with one important piece of advice.

Make sure you can get replacement parts!

    Most of the small and inexpensive helicopters usually come with an extra blade and other small parts but after that you are on your own. This is not usually a big deal because if you spent $20 bucks on something and you get a few months out of it and it breaks, you're not out a lot. So don't really sweat the inexpensive purchases!

But when you start spending $50, $60 or $100 or more on your RC helicopter you don't want to throw it away because you broke a $2 rotor blade or lost a tiny plastic part!

The good news is there are a lot of places that can supply you with replacement parts. Amazon sells a lot of replacement parts and you can usually find them when you are looking for a helicopter under the "People who bought this usually buy...." section of their sales page. But there are other websites that offer replacement parts from several manufacturers. Don't expect to find parts for the cheap $10 models sold in toy stores, though. Many of them are sold as throw always and are not meant for service or repair. You just buy another one.

HINT: Sometimes you might purchase a second whole helicopter for use as a source of parts for the cheap copters. This way you will have one to fly and the other to "cannibalize" for parts!

What I recommend is that you do a few searches to see which copters you like. Then see if where you purchase the copter also sells parts. If they do, you're good to go. If they don't search under the manufacturers name and find dealers who sell parts. If you can find some, you are good to go as well. The main focus should be to make sure you can get parts for any medium or high priced helicopter you are thinking of buying.

Also, always check with Amazon before you buy. First of all, their prices on remote control RC helicopters are very good and sometimes you can even get free shipping! But the best part about the Amazon site is that you can read reviews from other people that purchased that helicopter and read what they thought of it. This is great information. You will always find a few people that hate everything but if you find a lot of positive reviews, that can help you decide which model to buy.

RC Helicoptering is a very personal hobby and one that is built around what is fun to fly and what appeals to the flyer. Just take a few moments to make sure you can get replacement parts for what you want to buy and you will be prepared for years of happy flying!

Please do not take this for an endorsement of any kind because that is not how this was intended. You can choose any retailer that has a history of supporting the products they sell and that is known for quality customer satisfaction.

But still check with Amazon if only to read the reviews which will give you a unique insight into what you are buying instead of relying on what the manufacturer tells you.

Kit or Ready to Fly?

If you are like me, you like to build things with your hands. I have every tool known to man and have done jobs from simple light switch replacements to building an entire extension on my house including all plumbing and electrical. As I said, I like building and fixing stuff. But that doesn't mean that everyone should be the same way.

Every hobby has kits to let you build your own helicopter, airplane, race car, boat, etc. If it has a motor or engine, there's a kit available for it. But that doesn't mean that is the right way to go. There are times when kits are really cool and there are times when ready to fly are the best choices. Here is a little information that helps you make the right choice.

Kits

Kits are great ways to get really involved in your hobby. You can make your helicopter your own and customize your design, the way it flies and other things.

But you should really think twice about a kit if you are just entering the hobby. Why? Because kits are generally on the more expensive side and you do not want to learn on an expensive helicopter. You want to crash the $30 copter not the $300 one! You want to learn on a cheaper one so that when you crash (not IF you crash but WHEN you crash) it will dust itself off and go up in the air again! If you do a really bad crash, you are out only a few bucks and you buy another copter and learn from your mistakes.

Kits also give you an in-depth look at how the copter is put together so when you have to replace parts, you will know how to take it apart to get to those parts. This way you can fix it yourself instead of paying someone else to do it for you. Kits usually come with a replacement parts list as well so getting more parts in the future is easier. There is something to be said about knowing how to fix your own copter. Especially if you are away from home and flying and something goes wrong. You can just open the parts case, replace the part and be back in the air! No wasted trip or wasted days!

Now for the downside of kit building...........

You have to know pretty much what you are doing when you build a remote control RC helicopter or plane. If you mess up a car of boat, no big deal. But if you do something wrong with a plane or a copter and you crash it from 50 feet that could be a big deal. So give yourself an honest appraisal about your skills and decide if building a copter is right for you.

You will also need tools to build your kit. Chances are you will need to purchase some miniature screwdrivers and other tools to work with the small parts. Do not try to force larger tools in to this job because you will just strip screw heads and damage parts. Use the right tools for the right job. You can find miniature tools in hobby stores or on Amazon. They are not expensive. If you think you will enjoy building a copter kit, invest in some tools.

As you are building your kit, read the damned manual and follow it. Guys, this is not the time for the macho "men don't need instructions" crap. You DO need instructions! Follow them to the letter and test things out frequently. If something doesn't move freely and smoothly, correct it before moving on. The last thing you want is something binding up in mid air and watching your $300 kit come crashing down! Follow the instructions, check things frequently and use the right tools and you will be better off!

When it comes to flying your kit for the first time, take it slow and low.

Don't take it up high until you have gone through all the maneuvers and confirmed it is doing what it should. If something doesn't feel or work right, check it out and make the repairs or adjustments before proceeding.

RTF (Ready to Fly)

For those of you who want to get your new radio controlled RC helicopter and get right to flying, RTF units are the way to go.

Just unpack them, charge them, and get them in the air. You can go from unwrapping to flying in about 30-40 minutes with an RTF!

Ready to fly units come completely assembled so you can enjoy flying with almost no mechanical skill and no tools. Most micro and mini sized units come all ready to go because they are so small most people might have trouble working with such small parts. But you can also get RTF units in larger sizes as well. RTF units are great starter units and are also great for people with little or no mechanical desire to build anything.

All this being said, there is no doubt that flying something you built with your own two hands can be very rewarding. If that is your thing, dive right in and try your hand at building your own copter. But learn to fly first with one of the less expensive models.

When it Comes to Price.......

As with any hobby, Remote Control RC Helicopters are not free. But they are not expensive either and there are a few things you can do to save yourself some money.

On another page we spoke about the need to be able to purchase replacement parts and that should be a major consideration when buying any remote control RC Helicopter. After all, what good is a great price if you can only fly it once or twice before a part breaks and you have to throw it away?

But when you do find a model you like, and you determine that you can get replacement parts when you need them, then we need to look for the best possible value. Notice I said "value" and not price because those are two very different things.

Price is just the amount of money you pay for what you buy and that is important. But if you get a great price and the item arrives wrong, or damaged, or not at all, then where you buy it becomes very important as well.

I live in a large metropolitan area and there are hobby shops and malls in every direction. So it is no big deal to hit a few places to see who has the best deal on whatever it is I want to buy. Helicopters are no exception. I made the rounds and go what I thought were great prices.

Buying locally has some advantages. You get what you want right away and you actually can see, touch and feel what you are buying. If you are a fan of instant gratification, like most of us are, then buying locally is a good thing!

Another advantage is that you can return the item for service or assistance when you have a problem. If the unit is defective you can it another one, often the same day. That can be an advantage as well.

In my case, I got my local prices and then went online to check out how much I could buy them for elsewhere. The prices I thought were pretty reasonable I found were indeed very high. For example, one small "beginners" helicopter I could buy locally for $49.95 I found online for about $24.99! That was half the price! Another larger helicopter, which was being sold locally for $129.99, I found for $51.99!

Now I love instant gratification and patronizing my local retailers as much as anyone else, but when I can get so much more for my money online, I will take that route anytime! But here are a few bits of advice you should take into consideration:

First of all, know who you are buying from. If you are getting a great deal from someone who sell helicopters out of his garage, that might not be the best way to go. Anyone today can have a professional looking website for a few dollars a month so be careful. If the prices are close, buy from an established and well known business. You are more likely to get what you want and have support when you need it.

Second, go through their website and make sure you are buying new and not used or "REFURBISHED" materials or products. Look all over for the fine print or any disclaimers. If you see a price that is much less than everyone else, that's a red flag! I always look for prices that are comparable and am very suspicious whenever I see someone selling something for half of what everyone else is charging.

Use a credit card for your purchase. Your credit card company can stop payment and issue refunds when the retailer themselves refuse. The credit card company wants to keep you business and wants to protect themselves as well. They will act on your behalf and protect you.

Watch out for shipping scams as well. If you see a $100 remote control RC helicopter for $29.95 that might seem like a great deal. But if they are charging your $75 in shipping and handling, that ruins the deal. That is an inflated example but always include shipping and handling in the total price when making your decision.

I like EBAY and have got some great deals there but keep in mind that you are not dealing with only established businesses when you purchase there. You can be buying from individuals selling used or stolen merchandise as well as legitimate businesses. Look, most of the people selling on EBAY are good and honest people. But there will always be a few people looking to cheat you so be very careful. Look to see how many transactions they have had and what their rating is.

We will be spending an entire page on Amazon.com which is where I think you get the greatest overall value for your money but for now, just make sure you protect yourself and do your research before you purchase your first or next remote control RC helicopter. This is a great hobby when you get the best value for your money!

One Very Good

Place to Buy!

When it comes to purchasing your remote control RC helicopter, or anything else for that matter, online, there are a few things you should consider.

First, is the seller reputable? If you search under remote control RC helicopters you will find a tone of results and a lot of these are from businesses or websites you never heard of before. This does not mean they are bad or not reputable, but it should make you think a little bit about what will happen after you send your payment. It is likely the business won't be around the block or even in your town. So, if something goes wrong, who do you contact and how do you contact them?

Second, what kind of guarantee does the site offer and how do you go about reporting an issue or claim? What is their return policy and how does it compare to other sites selling similar products? How easy do they make it to return purchases?

Third, what about selection? If you go on a site that sells just XYZ Remote Control RC Helicopters, then you will see all of that brands models but nothing else.

You will hear only how great that manufacturer is and all comments or reviews will be biased towards that manufacturer. You want somewhere that sells a lot of different brands.

Fourth, and most people do not think about this; "How motivated is the seller to make you happy?" They might be the kind of business who wants to sell you one product, get the highest prices and deliver the lowest service and not care if you come back or not. Surprisingly, there are a lot of businesses that use this same business model!

When you take into consideration all of these factors, one website comes out far ahead. Amazon.com. Why? Here are just a few of the many reasons:

Amazon is HUGE and they sell EVERYTHING! They want you to come back to them again and again. In fact, their entire business model is focused on providing the best possible service and value so people do come back time and time again. They have a huge interest in keeping you happy because their future business depends on that! So they will do everything they can to make you happy.

Amazon also has a great selection. For private sellers to major retailers, you will find pages of items meeting your search criteria

. For helicopters, you will find large and small and from many different manufacturers. So you can easily go from one to the other and compare features and prices and other things to make sure you make the best purchase! It saves a ton of time! Plus, another really cool thing is that they will show you other similar products that people who purchased what you are looking at also purchased. For example, you are looking at a new helicopter. Amazon will also show you replacement parts kits, extra batteries and other similar models to make sure you get what you really want.

The prices at Amazon sometimes make you scour the fine print trying to find out what the catch is. But the fact is you will usually find the best possible prices at Amazon for a few reasons. First, remember the business model we just mentioned? Amazon wants you to come to them FIRST because you know their prices are great. Second, remember when we said they sell products for thousands of retailers? Well, these retailers know their listings will show up right along-side or their competition so their prices have to be low to get sales! For some, it is worth selling something at an extremely low cost just to get a new customer! You get a great deal and they get a new customer. It's works for everyone!

When it comes to after sales support, Amazon really shines! They have several shipping options from next day delivery for people who can't wait to get their copters in the air to economy shipping to meet every budget. In c=some cases, you can even get free shipping!

Returns are easy and disputes are rare. But if you have a problem that the retailer will not handle, Amazon will help you and believe me, they carry a HUGE weight with a retailer. Think about it. If you are unhappy, the business loses a customer. So they might not really go out of their way to make you happy. But if AMAZON is unhappy, they stand to lose a HUGE chunk of their business and they will do anything to keep that from happening! Well, maybe not anything, but close to it!

This means you have several layers of protection. You are buying from a large and well respected retailer. You are choosing from a large and varied selection. You have Amazon behind you if there is a problem and you get quick shipping as well. Also remember that your credit card company also provides you with protection on your purchases as well. So you can get what you want, get it at the best price, and buy with confidence.

But we have saved the very best for last..........

I hate hype. Every ad you read claims their products are the very best and they do everything perfectly and by the time you are done you wonder how the heck you managed to live without it for so long.

That's what ads are designed to do. Get you to buy THEIR products. But they don't tell you the truth. At least a lot of them don't.

Amazon, however, lets people actually write reviews of the product that you are thinking about buying.

Real reviews, not phony ones. You will see good reviews and you will see bad reviews as well. All honest. Negative reviews are not discarded or edited to make the product appear to be better than it really is. Like we said above, Amazon wants you to be happy. They WANT you to get the best deal and the best product. They would rather lose a sale than sell you something you are not happy with!

I was looking at one remote control RC helicopter and was close to buying it until I read the reviews. Bad reviews outnumbered good reviews by about 4 to 1. After reading the reviews I decided against that model and did some more shopping. I found another model with a lot better reviews and have been very happy with it. So the reviews helped me get a better product that I was happier with.

Ordering is easy too! After you order the first time and your information is already entered, you can buy anything with their "one clicks ordering" system. You literally can complete a purchase in less than 15 seconds! I mean it just doesn't get any easier. I have used Amazon for my helicopter purchases (and saved a bundle!) as well as home repair items, furnishing, sporting goods, just about anything! Once you give it a try I am sure you will agree with me. There is just no better place to buy your RC helicopter than through Amazon.com!

Even if you just visit Amazon to check out the reviews on what you want to buy it is very worthwhile. You can save yourself a lot of money and trouble by spending a few minutes on Amazon!

Please understand that we have nothing to gain by recommending any one site over another. We make no commissions or receive any compensation for recommending anyone. We rely strictly on personal experience.

Wherever you buy, just make sure to do your research and make sure the business is reputable.

Helicopter Safety

A remote control helicopter is one of the most dangerous RC devices. The rotating blades can inflict serious injury if you get too close or if you are too near a crash. The blades can cut your fingers or become dangerous projectiles if they break during a crash.

This chapter is a HIGHLIGHT of safety procedures. It does NOT contain everything you need to know or do under all circumstances. In other words, use common sense, think before you act, and be careful. Be considerate of others and take their safety into consideration as well. If there is the slightest doubt when it comes to safety DON'T DO IT!

Now that we understand each other, here are a few things you really need to think about and do each and every time you take your helicopter out to fly:

First of all, as we said RC helicopters have moving parts that can inflict serious injury so try and fly in areas where there are no people around.

Crowded parks are not good places for flying airplanes! Pick out a site and go when there are no other people around. Helicopters tend to attract attention and you do not want a crowd building around you when you are flying!

Second, don't bring your dog or other pets with you. You need to concentrate without distractions. You cannot watch your dog or cat and follow the copter at the same time. While it is not my intention to group together pets and your children, do not bring them along with you either especially in the beginning when you are learning. You need to concentrate and small children make that almost impossible. As they become older and want to seriously learn to fly, that might be different. In the beginning, though, they are best left at home.

Third, areas with other people's dogs and pets are not good areas as well. Dogs will tend to attack a helicopter and serious injury to the pet from the spinning blades could easily result. Move to an area where there are no pets or people!

Fourth, pick out a small area, say 20 ft by 20 ft and keep your copter confined to that area while you are learning. You need to be able to learn to control the copter in small places before you send it out further.

Fifth, ALWAYS, do a pre-flight check on all moving parts and hardware. Check for loose screws and broken pieces.

There is a lot of vibration, especially in gas helicopters, and fasteners can loosen quickly. It makes no difference if the copter flew perfectly last time out, ALWAYS do a preflight check. This can help you avoid damage to the copter and others around you.

Six, learn to use your eyes and ears before, during, and after flying. Listen for unusual or different noises. If you hear grinding or others sounds that weren't there before, stop everything and check it out. It is better to find a problem now instead of 100 feet in the air. Spotting a problem early can also save you a lot in broken parts and burned out motors.

Finally, and this is the most important:

Read the damned manual that came with your copter. Whether you have been flying for 15 seconds or 15 years, every copter could be different in how it flies and how it is put together. Do NOT assume you know how to fly it, build it, maintain, it, charge it or anything else. The manual came with it for a reason, READ IT and follow its instructions!!!!

Also, use the chargers and electrical components that came with your copter. Just because a charger or batter looks the same does not mean it is the same. Using the wrong charger could ruin a good battery and even cause a fire or explosion! Using the wrong battery could damage the copter, hand controller or both.

Weather

Excuse us for talking about this because a lot of it might seem to be common sense. But we really need to talk about weather and how it affects flying and safety. Understanding weather will make you a better flyer and a safer one as well!

The primary concern all RC helicopter fliers have when it comes to weather is wind. A windy day is not the time for even a seasoned flier to take out his copter for a fun time! Wind can cause stability problems and even crashes so be careful.

Wind can take even a large RC helicopter and cause it to fall, change direction or become unstable. When this occurs you may or may not be able to control the helicopter and your copter may crash. If there are other people around this presents a safety issue and you should not fly in any case.

Beginning pilots should only fly when it is dead calm out. Even on calm days you can get a gust every now and then but you can learn to control those over time. But constant wind does not make for an enjoyable time.

Generally speaking, the smaller your copter is the more prone it is going to be to wind. The heavier copters will be more stable but even the largest copter will be moved around easily by a good gust of wind. The small micro copters that are designed for flights indoors should never be flown outside because any breeze will toss them around like tissue paper. Some are so small that if someone sneezes in the next country you'll lose your copter!

Rain is another enemy. It will cause rust on metal parts and most of the time water and electronics really do not get along all that well together. If you should be in the sir and it starts raining, do a controlled landing and dry off as much of the copter and controller as possible when you get home.

If you see lightning or hear thunder, get the helicopter down and go home. You do not want to risk yourself or your copter. It's just not worth it. I don't know of anyone who got hit by lightning or lost a copter and thought it was still a great day!

When it comes to temperatures, follow the suggestions in your owner's manual. Lower temps can make linkages and mechanical systems slower and more sluggish. This will affect the handling and control of the copter. I make it a personal policy never to take my copter out when it is below freezing. I do that to protect the battery from freezing.

Speaking of batteries, lower temperatures will tend to shorten flying time so take that into consideration.

If you normally get 10 minutes at 80 degrees you might only get 5 minutes at 40 degrees. You do not want to realize this when the copter is 100 feet in the air!

Though technically not weather, I do not like to fly any copter at night. Even if it has lights on it you really cannot see it all that well and you cannot see other stuff around you either. Your depth perception goes way down at night as well. Stick to flying during daylight hours.

Your First Flight

First of all, welcome to the world of remote control RC helicopters. You have chosen a great fun-filled hobby that will likely stay with you for years! In order to get the most out of remote control helicoptering, let's get you started right so you get the most from your first flight.

To begin with, if this is your first time with remote control helicopters, start small. The last thing you want to do is start with a huge, expensive helicopter and watch it plummet to the ground because you hit the wrong button on the remote! Small helicopter are very lightweight and will take a ton of abuse without damage. Larger units are far less forgiving.

Small helicopters have different levels of quality however and small should not mean really, really cheap. The helicopters you see in catalogs for $10-15 will not be good to learn on as they are very limited as far as control and abilities are concerned. You want an inexpensive helicopter that will still give you the control you need to practice and prepare for the big boys! One suggestion is to look and purchase an inexpensive small helicopter with a built in gyro and two sets of blades. There should also be a tail rotor blade facing upwards as well. If you can find an inexpensive helicopter with all these features, that is a good place to start.

Most of the really small helicopters are designed for indoor use but don't let that stop you. You can have a heck of a lot of fun with a small copter inside the house. You can practice take offs and landings and basic movements like hovering and going up and down in a controlled manner. Then you can work on going forward and backwards, in a rectangle and finally in a circle. You can do all this without worrying about crashing. Because you will crash! A lot at first but you will get better as time goes on. The best part is that with the little helicopters you can crash and then just pick it up and start again!

Most of the smaller helicopters will charge directly from the remote control but a few have USB cables where you can charge from your computer. If you are purchasing one of those also make sure you can charge it from your remote or another source. Since most of these helicopters will fly for only about 5-8 minutes, you want to be able to charge it wherever you are!

Lastly, before you get started, don't take your small helicopter outside to fly. First of all, they are so light any wind will cause it to move around in an uncontrolled manner. You could lose your copter in a tree and not be able to do anything about it. Second, some of the smaller ones are infra red controlled and taking them out in sunlight often will not work. If you take them out and it's cloudy but the sun comes out in the middle of a flight you could be in trouble. The little guys are designed for in house use and that's where you should keep them!

Learning How to Fly –
Part 1

Learning how to fly an RC helicopter is harder than most RC devices but it is not too bad if you adopt a certain attitude and approach. If you try to do too much too quickly you will be heading back to wherever you bought your copter to either get a new one or buy some replacement parts. But if you take some care and use some patience, you'll be airborne shortly.

In this section we are going to go over some basics just so everyone is on the same page. We will take nothing for granted as even when we know something already it is good to be reminded every once in a while.

First, if you have never flown an RC copter before, make sure you get the right copter for your first one. I don't care if you're a millionaire or just hit the lottery, start with an inexpensive copter. Preferably a two bladed coaxial model which most of the cheaper ones are. These are the easiest to fly and are great for beginners.

The larger single blade models are the most expensive and also the most difficult to fly. Granted you can do more with them but when you are starting, you will not be able to do advanced moves anyway. So why place an expensive copter in harm's way when a $30 one will suit you just fine?

Regardless of what copter you buy or what skill level you currently are at, remember the purpose of all of this is to relax and have fun. That means enjoying what you are doing and not getting too stressed out or frustrated. So, in other words, take it slow, be patient, and have some fun.

Step One: Read Your Manual & Documentation

Contrary to what a lot of guys say, directions are provided for a purpose. The manuals are there to show you the correct way to operate whatever you purchased. They are also there to show you how to use your item safely and properly and how to get the best results.

Don't be a know-it-all. Every copter can be different and every copter has its own set of procedures and directions. Take the time to read about them. Enjoy the process and think of it as opening up a new world for you and get in the habit of learning all you can.

Make it a point to check all documentation and look for addendums to manuals, safety notices, and other important literature. This can save you time and money later on so invest the time now.

When you are done place all your paperwork in a folder and hopefully be able to take it with you when you go flying so you can refer to it as needed.

Step Two: Test, Test, Test

Just because you bought something new does not mean it is perfect out of the box. Even if your copter flew perfectly last time does not mean something didn't happen on the ride home or while it was in storage. ALWAYS do a preflight test to make sure everything is working properly.

Check all parts for wear or breakage and check to make sure no screws are loose or missing and that everything looks like it should. Make sure batteries are charged and connections are tight.

Then start up the copter and advance the throttle slightly. Not enough to lift off but enough to listen for problems. Check all servos and listen for odd noises. A little time spent now will help you discover problems that could otherwise show up 100 feet in the air.

If you find something wrong, STOP AND FIX IT! Do not tell yourself you'll fix it next time. Fix it now! Even if you have to scrub the flight and go to the hobby store for parts! Fixing problems on the ground are cheaper than fixing them after they break and cause a crash!

Step 3: Pick the Right Area

Helicopters are serious devices and their high spinning blades can cause severe injury.

Fly your copter where there are no other people around. Pick an area free of distractions as well so you can concentrate on what you are doing.

If there are a lot of people or pets around, find somewhere else or come back later and check again. It is not worth risking the safety of others just so you can have some fun. For more, check out the page on helicopter security.

The ground you are flying on should be flat. Helicopters are not that steady or stable right off the ground and will tend to lift off unevenly so you want to start on level ground. The same goes for landing as well.

There should be very few trees, no overhead power lines or other obstacles to get in your way and cause crashes. Just like kites, helicopters are often drawn towards trees and other places where they can get tangled or crash.

Step 4: Do you Pre-Flight Adjustments and Checklist

If you manual calls for any adjustments to be checked or made prior to flight, do it before you take off. If there is a checklist to follow, follow it. We strongly suggest you create your own checklist to make sure you do everything you are supposed to do. Eventually this will become habit but until that happens; a checklist is a great tool to use.

Step 5: Turning on the Copter

Follow the sequence described in your manual and turn on the copter and controller. Increase blade speed to where the copter is light on its base but not airborne yet.

Lower the speed and do this a few times. Note to see if the copter is moving around in either direction and see if there are adjustments that need to be made.

Step 6: Lift Off! (Slightly)

Increase the blade speed until you are just an inch or so off the ground and work on keeping the copter in one place. Adjust trim and other adjustments to keep the copter stable. Two bladed copters are much easier to do this with. Single bale models with tail rotors will require joystick control to stabilize the copter and you will need to work on this.

We have been told that some copters will require more rotor speed and faster speed increase than others. If you advance the rotor speed and your copter falls over, then increase SLIGHTLY faster but keep things under control at all times.

Raise and lower the copter several times and practice holding it as steady and still as possible. This will take some work at first but then it will get easier. It is helpful to do this at low altitude now because when you have the copter up high, you will not have time to think about what to do to control it, you will have to do it automatically.

Do this until you can keep the copter aloft an inch or so and steady for the duration of an entire battery pack. Practice take offs and landings and practice doing them gently. Do not shut off the throttle when something goes wrong and let the copter drop. Though this is not a big deal from an inch or so, dropping it from 30 feet is not advisable!

Practice all these steps several times and go through several battery packs in the process. Keep at it until all of this is automatic and you can do it without thinking. When you reach that point, we can head on to part 2!

Learning How to Fly –

Part 2

Now that you have mastered the basics and can get your helicopter to stay in one place hovering a few inches or so off the ground, it is time to get a little more daring and a little more complicated. But let's just make sure you have done everything in part one and are comfortable with everything. If you are not, stop and go back to the exercises in part one. These skills are critical to keep your copter in the air and minimize crashes and damage. Do NOT go on until you feel confident!

Step One: Controlling Your Copter

Speed and height are worth nothing unless you can control where your helicopter goes and how it gets to where it is going. If you can't control it, you will crash it or lose it!

Mark off an area about 15 feet by 20 feet for most mid-sized helicopters and larger for the big boys!

Practice hovering and landing your helicopter inside this area. Make smaller boxes and practice taking off from one box and landing in another. Always keep the helicopter within the marked off area.

Fly it around the edges making turns at the corners. Speed is not important, control is. If you have a two blade copter this will be easier but the larger helicopters with a tail rotor will be more difficult. Keep practicing until you can turn and control the helicopter and land in the boxes. Do this for at least two full battery packs. You should get so that everything becomes a habit and you can do it pretty much without thinking.

Step Two: More Control of Your Copter!

When you are comfortable flying forward within the box, try flying in reverse. Remember that flying in reverse means that some of the control will work backwards as well. Get used to flying forwards and backwards. There will be times in flight when you will have to fly backwards to get away from an obstacle or other object. Better to learn here than up there when that happens!

Step Three: Practice Turns

Now it's time to make wider turns while moving forward. That means turning the copter while it is moving forward or in reverse.

This will take some co-ordination between hands on your controller but it is not hard once you get the hang of it.

Step Four: Let Me Take You Higher!

Repeat the exercises we have talked about with your copter higher in the air. Try it about 3 ft off the ground, then 5 ft and higher. Always wait until you are comfortable at a certain height before going higher. Remember the higher you go the more damage a crash will bring. Take it slow.

Also keep in mind that the higher you go the more wind will become a factor. Wind will move your copter around and you need to be able to compensate for this with turns and speed.

Step Five: Longer Distance Flights

As you get comfortable with higher flight heights, you also need to get used to flying the copter further away from you. You need to get used to watching the copter as it gets smaller and still understanding where it is and how to get it where you want it.

This takes time and patience and experience. Do not rush this and force yourself. Remember this is supposed to be relaxing and fun! Some people are happy with small local flights and never fly it far from where they are. Others like to test the limits of the controller and go higher and farther. Neither is wrong, it is a personal preference.

Remember the controls will act differently when the copter is moving away from you than they do when the copter is moving towards you.

Turn controls will act the reverse way and you need to realize and understand this. Again, this comes with experience and patience.

All Steps: Easy Does It!

The controls used in flying helicopters are very sensitive. Make all movements slow and deliberate and do not do fast or violent actions. Speed should be gradually increased to raise the copter and gradually lowered to bring the copter down.

One common action is to dramatically reduce rotor speed when something unexpected happens. The result is a copter that is plummeting to the ground heading for a crash. Always bring the copter down slowly for a controlled descent to minimize damage and to land in a safe manner.

The faster the copter is moving the more sensitive the controls are likely to be. Because of this, take your time in getting used to the controls and their effects as you go faster and higher. Eventually you will get the "hang" of it and be able to control your radio controlled helicopter like a pro.

The Keys to flight Success!

Take it slow and do not proceed to the next step before you are comfortable with the preceding step. Each step is important to learn and master. If you give yourself time you will become a much better pilot!

Take it slow! Slow ascent (rise) and a slow controlled descent (landing) is the best way to minimize damage and control movements.

Become comfortable with all actions and maneuvers at lower heights before going higher.

Read your manual and follow their directions. They know best!

Always do a pre-flight checklist and fly only in suitable weather.

Batteries, Fuel & Accessories

Part of the fun with any hobby is making it your own. People customize their cars, their homes, their toys, just about anything they own just to make it "their own". Helicopters are no different. There are a ton of things people do to make their copters exactly how they want them to be.

While this is a fun part of the hobby, we must be careful so that we do not alter the flight characteristics of the copter by adding or changing parts and pieces. Helicopters are built to be balanced both front to back and side to side. Adding weight in any area of the copter may changes its flight characteristics as well as flight time.

Any weight change on the copter can affect flight time. The more the copter weighs, the more energy will be required to not only lift it into the air but keep it there as well.

This may reduce your flight time that you get out of your batteries.

For example, if you add something to your copter you might get 7 minutes instead of 8 out of your battery. While this is not a huge issue in most cases, it is something you should be aware of. Naturally, the more weight you add the more effect it will have.

Adding parts to your copter should only be done by someone who is knowledgeable in flying and building copters. In some cases, just adding a bunch of stickers to the body could shift the weight and alter the flying characteristics. While that is unlikely, it can happen. Most of the time changes in the body style or appearance will have the most impact.

Sometimes manufacturers will offer different accessories and body parts for their copters. In these cases the parts are usually designed for a particular model copter. If you have a different model, check with the manufacturer to make sure you can use that part. This is not a case of "I can make this fit so it will work"!

When it comes to batteries, make sure you use only the type designated by your owner's manual. You MUST match the voltage of the battery. Using a higher voltage battery will NOT give you better performance and will likely damage the electronics in the copter or controller. The current rating, usually given in MA is a measurement of how much power can be stored and delivered by the battery. In this case, the larger the MA rating, the longer the flight time.

There are also different types of batteries as well. You can have Lithium Ion, other forms of lithium and ni-cad batteries. Each has their own pluses and minuses and you should stick with the type that came with your copter. Changing battery type can have an effect on flight time as well as how the battery performs at the end of its charge. You do NOT want a battery that puts out full power until the very end and just dies. A free fall from 100 feet is bound to hurt!

Aftermarket or third party batteries may provide you with some savings but be careful about their size and weight and the connectors they use. If you have to change connectors, be very careful about which wire you connect to which terminal on the connecter. You must have the correct wiring you the copter will not fly and you will likely damage something. It is good practice to check the wiring with a volt meter when you are done. Compare the voltage and polarity against a known "good" battery to confirm.

Some batteries made by others will weigh more and have different size than the original. That might cause the battery not to fit properly or throw off the balance of the copter. Always get the closest match to the original battery as possible unless you are well versed in modifying the body to accept a larger battery.

When it comes to changing rotor blades or any other mechanical moving part, try to use exact manufacturers parts designated as being compatible with your copter.

With rotor blades size, shape and weight are critical and changing any of those can have a HUGE effect on performance and stability. Being "close enough" sometimes is not close enough. Gears, bearings and other chassis parts are best left to original manufacturer parts whenever possible.

Whenever you add or change anything on any helicopter, it is strongly advised that you go through the entire new flier training program listed in this book. This will enable you to check out how the copter flies and responds to controls after the changes. Better to find out at one inch off the ground than 30 feet. Take everything slow and go through all the movements and controls to make sure everything works properly.

If you have added or changed parts, pay special attention to hovering. This is where weight issues or problems will reveal themselves. Also check forward speed as additional weight in the front or rear can have a significant impact on speed.

In closing, just let me say that I encourage people to make their copters "their own" as long as they are careful and stick to what makes the copters fly properly and safely. If you are not sure about whether or not you can do a particular modification, talk to someone about it. If there is a store in your town that sells RC Helicopters, stop in and ask them. They are usually eager to help and spread their knowledge. After all, you could become their best customer!

Be smart, be careful and test out your copter after doing any repair or modification. This even applies to "official" modifications or applying factory replacement parts. Sometimes even small weight or position differences can have a huge effect on performance and handling.

Types of Electric Motors

This chapter is about as technical as you can get for most of us. Frankly, unless you want to get involved with the type of motors and replacing motors and such you really could skip this chapter all together if you want. But there are a few things you might want to know that could help you down the road. With all of that in mind, let's get technical!

There are two basic types of motors in all electric RC helicopters. These are brushless motors and brush motors. The brushless motors are the newer breed of motors and are more efficient and longer lasting than the brush type motors.

While that doesn't necessarily mean a copter using a brush type motor is bad, you should be aware that brush type motors are "old school" and have been around for decades. They do have brushes in them and they can wear out but that is pretty far down the road.

Unless you are spending a ton of money on a state of the art huge copter, I wouldn't worry about wearing out some brushes on an inexpensive copter. Still brushless is the latest and best technology.

Keep in mind that on the inexpensive copters the type of motor is a minimal concern and really should be down near the bottom of your list when it comes to choosing a cheaper copter. As you go up in price, it might play a larger factor. Though some people might disagree with me and pull out some technical studies and other information, I just feel that most helicopter motors are cheap and easy to replace so if it wears out, it is no big deal. If I find a copter I like, I'll buy it regardless of what type of motor it has.

But if I'm getting an inexpensive top of the line copter a few years down the road, I'll look more seriously into brushless. Again, this is neither right nor wrong but rather just my personal opinion.

Brushless motors have fewer moving parts and no brushes. Hence the name "brushless". This means there are no parts to wear down and no carbon mess inside the motor as the brushes wear down. There is also little or no break-in period required with brushless motors.

Brushless motors produce almost constant power regardless of speed and also produce more power for their size and weight than brush-type motors. However, brushless motors also require a controller which adds to the costs of building the copter.

As far as performance is concerned, you will get more out of a brushless motor but expect to pay for those benefits.

Although there are specific break-in instructions for brush type motors, I prefer to use some common sense regardless of what type motor you are using in your copter.

Any brand new motor should be operated at lower than normal speeds for a while at first. If you are just learning how to fly you will probably be doing this automatically as you learn. But if you are experienced, avoid taking the copter up like a rocket with a brand new motor. Fly it around low or just let it sit on the floor running for a while to seat the brushes or wear in the bearings.

Do you really have to do this? Probably not but it is good practice and takes only a little bit of time to protect your investment and get a longer life out of it. Proper break-in also is said to reduce heat and slightly improve efficiency as well. Nothing wrong with that, is there?

Some people like to play around with motors to get more power and more speed and longer flight time from their copters. While there is nothing wrong with that, it is out of the scope of this book as this is a book targeted for beginners who want to learn how to fly.

I will say that motors are rated in watts and horsepower and you should be careful when it comes to increasing either the size or the weight of the motor.

Both will affect flight and handling. There are several websites that have charts and formulas on how to determine motor size and power draw. This is very technical information so if you are into that kind of thing be sure to search under "electric RC helicopter motors" for more information and charts for different applications.

A site that offers calculators to assist you in choosing the right motor for your needs can be found at http://ecalc.ch

Gas & Nitro Engines

If you are intent on going large scale and also want realistic sounds and copter performance, then perhaps you should consider gas or nitro engines. These engines use fuel instead of electricity to power the copter.

The advantages are that they can fly longer than their electric counterparts and they can be refilled and go right back up in the air. There is not recharge time except for the servos.

The disadvantages are many. These engines are noisy, messy, and smelly and they vibrate a lot more than electric motors. They require more maintenance, you will need to clean and wipe the residue from the fuel off your copter, and they can be a bear to start at times. You will need a glow plug, fuel, a battery and other things just to get them started. Plus, these engines get HOT and can burn you if you are not careful.

Personally, I do not advise a beginner to get a gas or nitro copter. There is just too much to do to get it started and too many other things that are not particularly fun either.

Neighbors get annoyed if you practice in your back yard because of the noise. With electrics they won't hear much of anything!

In any case, here is some basic info on both gas and nitro engines:

Nitro engines use a glow plug that you heat up with a battery until it is hot enough to ignite the fuel. Then you spin the engine, it hopefully starts and keeps running until the fuel runs out. Lubrication is added to the fuel during manufacture to lubricate the engine.

Gas engines are the real "old school" engines that use a regular spark plug and a pre-mixed gas/oil mixture for fuel. Not sure if there are a lot of these around today as glow plug nitro engines are most common.

As we said, both of these engines are noisy and dirty and somewhat messy. You will be wiping down your copter after each use to remove the oil film that spews out of the engine. You cannot really use these in residential areas even to practice because they are loud and will disrupt the neighbors.

Personally I love the convenience of turning on a switch and taking off. I love the quiet of electrics as well and the clean air they help keep clean. I don't have any real desire to add to the realism by adding noise and dirt and mess to the equation. For me, flying copters should be fun and I don't really see the need to add all the hassle in place of even part of the fun. Because of all of this and more, I really do not recommend them to beginners. Until you feel the need, stick with a small or midsized electric.

For those interested in pursuing gas or nitro engines, there is a ton of information available online. Just search for it and you will find more than you will ever need!

Electronics and Servos

While you don't need to know much about the electronics in your copter, it does help to understand just how the thing works and how to get it to go up in the air and fly and land with some degree of control. With that in mind, here is a really short overview of the electronics in your remote control helicopter system:

Depending on what type of system you have, your controller communicates with your copter by means of radio waves (RF) or a beam of infra-red light (IR). We cover those systems in another chapter.

The biggest difference between the two systems is that IR is strictly line of site. That means the copter has to "see" the controller at all times. It cannot go through walls or around corners. RF systems, on the other hand, can go through walls, around corners and cover longer distances. Because IR systems use light to communicate, they are pretty much useless outside even in partial sunlight.

That is why large or mid-sized copters will always use RF technology.

The **controller is your transmitter** which means it transmits data to your copter. Inside the copter there is a **receiver** that takes that information and processes it. It turns the data into commands that tell the copter what you want it to do

. Somewhere on the copter there will be an antenna that receives the signals from the controller. Sometimes the antenna is visible and sometimes it is hidden within the structure of the copter.

Up until now all of this is happening electronically. But we need something that converts electronic signals into physical movements that control the helicopter. The parts that accomplish that are called **servos**.

Servos take electronic signals and turn them into physical movement. Servos will make linkages move, throttles advance and return and other instructions. Without servos nothing could work.

Controllers come with a certain number of channels. The minimum is usually 2 for the real cheap toy copters and 3 for the inexpensive "non toy" models. The number of channels for the more expensive copters can go as high as 6. The more channel the more things you can control. Each channel is usually designated to accomplish a certain movement. So the more channels you have, the more flexibility and control you will have over your copter in flight.

Since servos convert electronic information into physical movement, they are mechanical components and need to be able to move freely.

Anything that binds a servo will compromise flight and control.

Other electronics will include motor controllers, lights, and other electronic accessories such as cameras, etc. The more electronics that you have the larger battery you will need as well.

The on-board battery will be responsible for turning the main and tail rotor blades as well as powering the electronics. The majority of the power goes to the motors but you still need to power the electronics. In gas or nitro copters, you will still have a battery on board to power up and support the electronics. In reality, there are batteries in even non-electric copters.

There are also batteries in the controller as well. In the high end models these could be rechargeable but in most hobby aircraft they are just AA or AAA batteries. Because of the power and voltage needed, you could have 6-8 of those batteries.

It is important to use the type of batteries that your controller manufacturer designates. Many people like the reduced cost of rechargeable batteries and substitute ni-cad batteries for the regular type. If your manual says this is OK, that is fine. But it says not to use ni-cads, then don't. Ni-cads have a slightly lower voltage per battery than standard batteries.

Which means that when you have six batteries each with a lower voltage, then the voltage to the transmitter will be less as well. Many transmitters are designed to compensate for this but not all are. If in doubt, read your manual or contact the manufacturer.

With your controller and helicopter you will also have a battery charger. In high end units you might have one charger for the copter and one for the controller. In smaller or cheaper copters you charge the copter with a wire from the controller and use regular batteries. In these cases, no battery charger is provided or needed.

I have seen a couple of copters that charge through a USB cable through your computer. If you get one of those, invest in a USB charger that plugs in the wall. They are inexpensive and give you more choices when it comes to where to charge your copter.

If you are not going to fly your copter for a while, it is smart to remove the batteries from the controller. Old batteries can leak and damage the controller. If you store your gear outside where it can get below freezing that is not good for batteries either. Remove all batteries and bring them inside for the winter.

Although this might be common sense, it bears telling here. Only use the same voltage batteries that came with your copter. A 20 volt battery is NOT going to give you more flight time than the 10 volt battery that came with your copter! It will give you less time because it will likely damage or completely ruin the electronics and servos system.

STAY WITH THE VOLTAGE OF THE ORIGINAL EQUIPMENT BATTERY AT ALL TIMES!

You can, however, use a battery with a higher CURRENT rating. For example, a 1000ma battery will give you more flying time than a 500ma battery. Just make sure it is physically the same size and weight and that the voltage is the same as the original battery.

Some batteries are rated in watts and the higher the wattage the more power the battery will have. Always know and use the correct voltage though. That is ALWAYS the primary rule.

Electronics hate water, lightening and extreme heat. Servos dislike the extreme cold of winter as well. With all this I mind, do NOT fly your copter when it is raining, during a thunder storm under any circumstances, or during extreme heat or cold. This will prolong the life of both the copter and the pilot as well. If it is too hot or cold for the copter, it is usually too cold for the pilot as well!

Electronics are usually very reliable. Naturally they can be damaged in a crash so be sure to do a pre-flight check whenever you fly. The common problems with electronics are usually centered around the batteries and, in some cases, the servo system because it is electro-mechanical in nature.

The most common problem is usually loose connections between the servos or at the battery itself.

If a connection is loose it may make intermittent contact which could cause major problems in flight. Check all connections on a regular basis.

Another common problem would be corrosion at either the battery or one of the connections. You will see little white or yellow crystals at the terminals or sockets. When you see this, you might be able to salvage the copter by scraping off the contacts and then use a cotton swab dipped in a mixture of baking soda and water to clean off the contact.

If the corrosion was there for a long time the entire contact could be gone or severely damaged. If this should be your problem, you either replace the connector or the copter.

Batteries are known to leak as well and they leak acid which can damage you copter. Never let the battery freeze and do not overheat the battery by overcharging. Always use the right charger for the right battery. Don't assume that if two chargers look the same that they are the same. Check the ratings before using another charger.

Most of the time you will never even give the electronics much thought because they are so reliable. Just make sure to check connections, take care of the battery and use the copter as it was designed and the electronics should give you years of faithful service.

Crashes & Repairs

I don't care if you are brand new to RC helicopters or a seasoned vet with 50 years of flying. You are going to crash. It happens to everyone. Winds can kick up, parts can loosen or fail and stuff just happens. Granted it happens to the "newbie" a lot more often but it still happens to everyone no matter how good you are as a pilot.

When crashes do happen, you need to restore your copter to proper flying condition before you take it up again. Sometimes this is very easy and sometimes it requires a lot of time and money. We will discuss both scenarios here.

Hopefully you have read this book and followed the directions on how to fly and how to minimize crashes and damage during learning. If you didn't do that, we suggest you go back and read those parts before you start flying again. If you did read them, hopefully your damage is minimal.

Every helicopter flier should have some kind of spare parts box.

In the beginning this box will hold any parts that came with your copter plus any spare parts you may have purchased.

Keeping the parts in their own box will keep them organizes in one place so they will be easy to fly.

I suggest one of those plastic boxes you can get at a home center, or through Amazon.com that has smaller compartments within the large box. Some boxes have moveable dividers and that is even better. This way you can separate parts into their own compartments and make them easier to find. Some parts are very small and to pick them out of a large pile might prove difficult. Plus, having them separate and easily identifiable allows you to see when you are running low or out and get new ones on order before you need them.

If you have more than one helicopter, you might wish to have more than one pats box and label each box with the type of helicopter that those parts are for. This is because some parts look almost the same but might be slightly different in shape or weight and cause problems. Be organized and it will help you a lot!

The most important thing is to make it a habit to fix problems NOW and not wait until later. If something is slightly loose, tighten it now before taking the helicopter in the air. A loose part now could loosen further and fall off in mid flight and cause all kinds of nasty problems.

Even though it might mean cancelling a day's flight, you are better off addressing things now and not later when it might be too late.

It also helps to have the right tools at your disposal. That means miniature screw drivers and pliers and other tools you might need to replace or remove parts. As you get more involved with your helicopters you will acquire some of these tools as you need them. But to start, a good set of miniature screw drivers and nut drivers along with some good Allen and hex wrenches will get you started. Also remember that most helicopters are made in china or Japan and likely will have metric fasteners so buy your tools accordingly.

Failure to have the right sized tools can and will result in stripped screw heads or hex heads and that can create a nightmare when it comes to removing those damaged fasteners.

When you buy your tools, stay away from those "dollar store" miniature tools as they will break and strip out fast. Go with a quality set and if you treat them well, they will last for years. Even the high quality sets are not real expensive so spend a few dollars more and buy some high quality tools. If it matters to you (or to your spouse!), these tools will have other uses around the house as well so you can justify the expense!

Whenever a part breaks or becomes missing, replace it with an original manufacturers part whenever possible. This will assume correct fit, correct weight, and proper flight characteristics.

Sometimes there may be differences you just can't see and you do not want to risk you copter to an inferior part.

Replacement parts can be purchased from a local deal or online source. Amazon.com has a wide array of parts for the copters they sell. Sometimes it is a great idea to purchase a parts kit when you buy your copter. These contain frequently needed rotor blades, tail blades, linkages and other parts. These kits cost about ten bucks or so and are well worth having. If you purchased a medium or large sized copter it is wise to get the parts kit. Eventually you WILL need some of those parts!

Rotor blades that have small nicks in them from crashes or hitting objects are usually OK to use unless they are really beat up. But if they have really deep gouges in them, consider replacement. The gouges can weaken the overall structure and cause a potentially dangerous situation. If that happens, I always replace both blades rather than just the one. You can save the old blade as an emergency replacement if it is not that bad.

Remember every dent or blemish on a main rotor can alter the way air flows over it and that will make the copter handle differently. Always examine blade condition before and after every flight.

DYI or Pay for Repairs?

One common question is whether or not a helicopter owner should or can repair their own copter.

The answer is both yes and no. I know some people who can fix almost anything and others who need to be told which end of the screwdriver you hold and which end goes on the screw.

If you have the mechanical ability to do your own repairs go for it. But remember that everything has the potential to alter flight characteristics and you need to install the right parts in the right manner and do all the adjustments necessary after certain part replacements.

I would say most of us can handle rotor blade replacements and batter replacements. Internal parts like gears and motors might be a little above some people though. The key is to know your limitations and do not exceed them. It is better to admit your skill limitation and pay for a repair rather than try it and lose a $400 copter because you forgot to do something during the replacement.

A good rule of thumb is how confident you feel about doing a particular repair. If you are not concerned or nervous at all, then go ahead and give it a try. If it is a little more involved there are several online forums for helicopter owners and fliers where you can ask questions and get some free advice. These forums are a great resource and you can learn a lot by just looking at them. It's kind of fun at the same time.

There is also no harm in taking your copter to a repair place and offer to pay someone to show you how to do something.

If what you need to know is a common repair, you can pay once, be shown how to do it, and from that point on you can do it yourself.

Pride should never be an issue when it comes to deciding who is going to fix or modify your copter. The entire hobby is built around enjoyment. If you enjoy working on your own copter, that's great. You will save both time and money. Money you can put towards bigger and better copters to fly!

But if you do not enjoy that sort of thing, there is no shame or harm in paying someone else to keep your copter in top condition.

Learning Without Risk

One of the most difficult periods for a new copter pilot is learning how to fly their new helicopter. They are nervous and afraid of crashing and damaging their helicopter. This fear is pretty widespread and hits just about everyone who comes into this hobby for the first time.

After all, no one wants to see their new "toy" break into a million pieces or crash 4 seconds into take off and break a main rotor. Yet these things do happen to both novice and experienced pilots frequently.

Fortunately there is something you can use to crash without damaging your equipment. That "something" is called a flight simulator. It is used in conjunction with your computer and allows you to use a pretty much standard controller and a computer software program to create a realistic flying experience.

Using the simulator you can lift off, hover, fly around and crash from any height without damaging your copter.

You can get used to the controls and start to develop "muscle memory" or, in other words, the habit of knowing what to do when something happens.

Flight simulators are available from several sources and they range from about $25-30 to over $300. Naturally there is more realism and features to the more expensive models but even the less expensive models will give you a certain amount of control and practice.

The whole point of the simulators is to get you used to what the controls do and how the helicopter reacts. Trying this on a computer screen where there are no blades to break, no copters to crumble after a 100 ft drop because you cut the throttle back to zero by mistake means that you can make mistakes without damaging anything.

You want to get to the point where you see something and you react without thinking. You want to get to the point where your hands and fingers know what to do without you telling them. Just like you now ride a bike or drive a car without thinking, a flight simulator will help you get that way with flying without all the damage in between.

If you join a model helicopter club, they may have one you can borrow to help you learn. Of course, they will also have someone there to teach you on an actual copter which is more fun!

While there is no substitute for actually flying you copter in real air on a real field, flight simulators do come somewhat close and will help you learn without spending a lot of time and cash buying replacement parts!

FREE R/C Hobby Information!

We would like to thank you for purchasing this book on radio controlled helicopters. To show our appreciation, we would like to send you a free report with some more information on R/C hobbying that will help you get more enjoyment from this great hobby.

There is no obligation on your part to get this free report. Just click on the link below, or copy and paste it into your web browser to access the webpage. It's our way of saying thank you and helping you get even more from your R/C experience!

http://www.howtomastery.com/radiocontrolled.html

Printed in Great Britain
by Amazon.co.uk, Ltd.,
Marston Gate.